Japanese HOME COOKING
with MASTER CHEF MURATA

Japanese
HOME
COOKING

with MASTER CHEF MURATA

60 Quick and Healthy Recipes

YOSHIHIRO MURATA

Photographs by Akira Saito

KODANSHA INTERNATIONAL
Tokyo • New York • London

Distributed in the United States by Kodansha America LLC, and in the
United Kingdom and continental Europe by Kodansha Europe Ltd.

Published by Kodansha International Ltd., 17-14 Otowa 1-chome,
Bunkyo-ku, Tokyo 112-8652

First edition, 2010
18 17 16 15 14 13 12 11 10   10 9 8 7 6 5 4 3 2 1

Library of Congress Cataloging-in-Publication Data

Murata, Yoshihiro.
  Japanese home cooking with Master Chef Murata : 60 quick and
healthy recipes / Yoshihiro Murata ; photographs by Akira Saito. -- 1st ed.
      p. cm.
  Includes index.
  ISBN 978-4-7700-3132-7
  1. Cookery, Japanese. 2. Quick and easy cookery. I. Title.
  TX724.5.J3M869 2010
  641.5952--dc22
                                2010007506

www.kodansha-intl.com

C O N T E N T S

CHAPTER **8** **SOUPS**   91

INTRODUCTION

This book is for anyone who has ever wanted to make Japanese food, but doesn't know where to start. Most of the recipes in this book require no special ingredients or unusual equipment. I wanted to provide recipes that use ingredients found at an ordinary supermarket.

In fact, Japanese cooking is really not that exotic. You probably have a bottle of soy sauce in your pantry. Soy sauce, essential to Japanese cooking, is made by steaming soybeans and roasted wheat into a mash, then fermenting the mash until it develops a rounded, meaty flavor. With soy sauce and sugar you can make authentic teriyaki sauce, and then all you have to do is grill or sauté beef, salmon, tofu, or any other ingredient you wish, and baste it with the sauce to make a satisfying dish.

Also, I have chosen recipes that do not strictly call for *dashi*, a basic fish stock made from dried bonito and *kombu* kelp. Most of the soups, simmered dishes, and hot pots call for chicken broth that can be bought at the supermarket. Even in Japan we often use chicken broth, usually in powder form, for many of these dishes. (For cooks who want to try it, I have included a method for making dashi and a few recipes that use it.)

The recipes in this book reflect authentic Japanese home cooking. I learned them from my father, my mother, and my grandmother. A few I picked up outside my home, when I tried something I thought was good and asked the cook for the recipe. I've put the recipes in my own words, but the dishes are all familiar favorites that Japanese know from their mothers' cooking.

At my restaurant, Kikunoi, in Kyoto, Japan, I serve *kaiseki* cuisine, which has its roots in the Buddhist monastic tea ceremony and has been continuously refined for centuries down to the present day. However, I have long believed that the food we ate at home as children, lovingly prepared by our mothers, is the truest and best cooking we know. Mothers adjust for each child's tastes and season with the utmost attention. It is the greatest effort a cook can put forth. As a professional chef, I must compete with other restaurants to provide outstanding meals, but I'm happiest when I know that I am cooking for a person who will truly enjoy what they eat.

Through the Japanese Culinary Academy, a nonprofit organization dedicated to teaching and promoting Japanese cuisine, I have invited many chefs from the West, China, and India to Japan, and I am often invited to other countries. I think that all chefs want to focus on their customers' needs, especially by providing more health-conscious meals, which is now a global trend. It seems that the most accomplished chefs are the ones most eager to learn something, even just a little bit, about healthy techniques and ingredients from Japanese cuisine.

The main reason for the healthiness of Japanese cuisine is because we don't rely on fat and oil for flavor, but instead try to bring out the natural *umami* in foods. Many ordinary foods have umami, the "fifth taste," which is different from saltiness or sweetness. Aged cheese and beef contain a lot of umami, as do ripe tomatoes and good wine. The dense savor of root vegetables or the subtle sweetness of raw fish are further examples of umami. Even types of salt vary in this respect: refined salt is just plain salty, but we Japanese prefer the more rounded flavor of natural sea salt because it has umami.

Of course, anyone can detect the taste of umami, even if they don't have a word for it. It is said that milk consists of sweetness, richness, and umami, which means that as mammals we are all programmed from birth to crave foods high in sugar, fat, and amino acids that provide umami. But in Japan, Buddhist strictures prevented us from eating meat or animal fats until the late nineteenth century; and refined sugar and other sweeteners were until recently too expensive for most Japanese to use. Therefore, Japanese cuisine has developed in a very different way from Western and other Asian cuisines: we satisfy our biological need for the flavors of milk by focusing on umami rather than fats and sweeteners.

We all wish to be healthier, but if you always dine out or buy takeout food, you'll never even get started. By cooking the same recipe repeatedly, and sometimes cooking for others (and sometimes making mistakes), the dishes you make will improve and you will cook with more confidence. As you cook more, you can add your own variations, widening your repertoire. Nothing will change if you don't challenge yourself. So, why not begin cooking healthy food at home? I assure you that with this book, you can cook Japanese food quickly and easily and develop a close feeling for the cuisine. It is my pleasure to help you, even if only a little bit, to lead a healthier life and make yourself and your loved ones happier.

Yoshihiro Murata

USING THIS BOOK

Standard U.S. measures are used throughout this book; the metric conversions in parentheses are also in accordance with U.S. standards.

- For fluid measures, 1 cup = 240 ml (rounded up from 236.59 ml).
- For weights, 1 ounce = 30 g (rounded up from 28.349 g).

A complete list of measurement conversions may be found on p. 111.

Please choose low-sodium or sodium-free chicken broth if available.

Microwave cooking times are for a 500-watt microwave oven. Lower-powered ovens will need longer cooking times.

CHAPTER 1

Salads

【*Aemono*】

The salads in this section are just examples; once you grasp the basic sauce and dressing recipes introduced here, you can easily create your own *aemono* using your favorite ingredients.

GREEN BEANS
WITH SESAME SAUCE

SERVES TWO

INGREDIENTS

6 oz. (170 g) young green beans

2 qts. (2 L) water for cooking green beans

1 tsp salt

Sesame dressing:

- 1 Tbsp toasted sesame seeds
- 1 tsp soy sauce
- 1 tsp sugar

Seasonal vegetables dressed with ground sesame seeds is a classic recipe with its roots in vegan Buddhist monastic cooking (known as *shojin* cuisine).

1 Bring the water and salt to a boil in large pot. Rinse the green beans, remove the stem ends and cut into about 1 ½ in. (4 cm) long pieces. Cook in the boiling water until tender but still crisp. Shock in cold water and drain well.

2 Chop the sesame seeds with a knife (if making a large batch you can use a food processor) and combine with the soy sauce and sugar in a medium bowl to make the sesame sauce. Dress the green beans with the sauce and mound on a serving dish.

FAVA BEANS
WITH SWEET TOFU SAUCE

SERVES TWO

INGREDIENTS

7 oz. (200 g) fresh fava beans, removed from pods but not skinned

2 qts. (2 L) water for cooking fava beans

1 tsp salt

Sweet tofu dressing:
- $\frac{1}{3}$ block (4 oz. / 120 g) firm tofu
- 1 tsp peanut butter
- 1 tsp sugar
- 1 tsp soy sauce

This tofu dressing also goes well with steamed shucked clams, cubes of grilled salmon, and even fruits like persimmon.

1 Bring the water and salt to a boil in large pot. Cook the fava beans in the boiling water until tender. Shock in cold water, drain, and slip the beans out of their skins. Set aside.

2 Wrap the block of tofu in several paper towels, place on a microwave-safe dish, and microwave for 1 minute in order to remove water from the tofu. Remove the paper towels.

3 Place the sugar, soy sauce and peanut butter in a medium bowl, add the tofu, and combine well by crushing the tofu and mixing with a rubber spatula. Add the fava beans to the bowl and toss with the tofu dressing.

SPINACH
WITH PEANUT SAUCE

INGREDIENTS

1 bunch fresh spinach, about 6 oz. (170 g)

Peanut dressing:

{ 2 Tbsp salted peanut butter

{ 1 tsp sugar

¼ cup (40 g) unsalted roasted peanuts, crushed, for topping

Sautéing spinach immediately after rinsing it leaves just the right amount of liquid in the cooked spinach to make a dressing with the peanut butter.

1 Trim off the roots of the spinach if attached, rinse in cold water and cut into 2 in. (5 cm) pieces. Heat a non-stick frying pan, add the spinach and cook over medium-low heat, stirring from time to time, until the stems of the spinach are tender but still crisp. Turn off the heat and leave in the pan until cooled to room temperature.

2 Combine the peanut butter and sugar in a medium bowl. Dress the spinach with the sauce and mound on a serving dish. Sprinkle with the crushed peanuts.

Put the peanuts in a plastic bag and crush with a rolling pin.

The water from the spinach thins the sauce to the right consistency.

DAIKON RADISH
WITH *WASABI*-SOY DRESSING

INGREDIENTS

3 in. (7.5 cm) length daikon *radish*, peeled (about 8 oz. / 230 g)

1/2 log (about 5 oz. / 140 g) kamaboko (or 12 *kanikama* imitation crab legs, thawed if frozen)

1/2 stick celery, chopped

Wasabi-soy dressing:

- 2 Tbsp wasabi paste
- 1 1/3 Tbsp soy sauce
- 1 1/3 Tbsp lemon juice
- 2 tsp sugar
- 1/2 Tbsp toasted sesame seeds

Thinly cut *daikon* can be eaten just as it is, shredded and tossed with dressing, but here I added *kamaboko*, a kind of fish cake, to give the dish a deeper flavor.

1 Peel the daikon and cut into thin sticks. Cut the kamaboko into thin sticks about the same size as the daikon sticks. (If using imitation crab legs, roughly shred them by hand. If the thawed meat is too watery, simply pat dry with a paper towel.) Combine the daikon, kamaboko, and celery in a large bowl and transfer to a serving bowl.

2 Combine all dressing ingredients in a small bowl. Just before serving, pour the dressing over the vegetables and toss.

ONION AND
CRISPY BACON SALAD

INGREDIENTS

1 onion (sweet, red, or yellow), peeled and thinly sliced

1 cup (33 g) lightly packed washed and trimmed radish sprouts

2 cups (80 g) lightly packed baby salad greens, washed

2 oz. (60 g) sliced bacon (about 2 regular slices), chopped

Peanut and *wasabi*-mayo dressing:

1 Tbsp salted peanut butter

1 Tbsp wasabi paste

1 Tbsp mayonnaise

1 Tbsp soy sauce

1 Tbsp lemon juice

1 Tbsp chopped scallion

2 tsp toasted sesame seeds

Onion salad makes a good side dish for grilled meats, and eating raw sliced onion is a refreshing way to clean the palate during a meal.

1 If using an ordinary strong-tasting onion such as a yellow onion, soak the slices in cold water for about 20 minutes, drain, and blot dry.

2 Cook the bacon in a frying pan over medium-low heat until crisp, about 10 minutes. Transfer to paper towels to drain.

3 Mix all dressing ingredients together in a small bowl. Arrange the onion, radish sprouts, and baby salad greens in a salad bowl and top with the bacon. Just before eating, pour the dressing over the vegetables and toss.

CHAPTER 2

Sautéed Dishes

【*Yakimono*】

This section includes some popular teriyaki dishes easily made at home. They are wonderful both as everyday meals and for entertaining friends. You need only an ordinary frying pan; non-stick works best.

BEEF TERIYAKI

INGREDIENTS

2 beefsteaks, 3 ½ oz. (100 g) each

1 Tbsp vegetable oil

Teriyaki sauce (mixed in advance):

   1 ½ Tbsp sugar

   3 Tbsp soy sauce

   6 Tbsp sake

2 tsp *wasabi* paste

Slivered lemon peel

1 cup (40 g) lightly packed baby salad
   greens, washed and spun dry

4 florets broccoli, blanched

Technically speaking, teriyaki is not really a sauce, but a grilling technique that uses sweetened soy sauce as a glaze. My recommendation for the best glaze is to use 1 part sugar, 2 parts soy sauce, and 4 parts *sake*.

1   Heat a frying pan over medium-high heat, add the oil, and sear the steaks on both sides until browned. Lower the heat to medium. Add the teriyaki sauce and simmer, shaking the pan from time to time and basting the steaks with a spoon, until the sauce thickens slightly and glazes the steaks, about 4 minutes.

2   Transfer the steaks to a cutting board and cut into ½ in. (1.5 cm) thick slices.

3   Arrange the steak slices on a serving plate and pour the sauce from the pan over. Top with the wasabi paste and slivered lemon peel. Place the baby salad greens and broccoli on the side.

Simmer the teriyaki sauce, being careful not to scorch the pan.

Baste the steaks from time to time to glaze them with the sauce.

TOFU TERIYAKI

INGREDIENTS

1 block firm tofu, about 12 oz. (340 g)

2 Tbsp cornstarch

1 Tbsp vegetable oil

Teriyaki sauce (mixed in advance):

{ 1 1/2 Tbsp sugar

3 Tbsp soy sauce

1/4 cup plus 2 Tbsp (90 ml) *sake*

1 small, green bell pepper (or any other sweet pepper such as Anaheim)

2 scallions, chopped

Crushed chili pepper (or *shichimi* spice powder)

1 cup (10 g) lightly packed dried bonito flakes (optional)

This is a great way to eat tofu. Be sure to sauté the tofu until the surface is browned, so it will not break apart quite as easily.

1 Dust the tofu with the cornstarch. Heat a large, non-stick frying pan over medium-high heat, add the oil, and sear the tofu on both sides until golden brown. Lower the heat to medium. Add the teriyaki sauce and bring to a simmer. Add the green pepper and continue to simmer, shaking the pan from time to time and basting the tofu with a spoon, until the sauce thickens and glazes the tofu, about 4 minutes.

2 Working carefully so as not to break it, transfer the tofu to a cutting board and cut into 1/2 in. (1.5 cm) thick slices.

3 Arrange the tofu slices and green peppers on a serving plate and pour the sauce from the pan over. Top with the chopped scallions and crushed chili pepper. Garnish with the dried bonito flakes, if desired.

PAN-GRILLED SKEWERED CHICKEN

SERVES TWO

Yakitori (grilled chicken) is popular at many Japanese eateries. It can easily be made at home in a frying pan.

INGREDIENTS

6 or more bamboo skewers

7 oz. (200 g) chicken thighs

7 oz. (200 g) chicken breast

1 medium green bell pepper or any sweet pepper, halved and seeded

2 fresh *shiitake* mushrooms, cleaned, stems removed

¼ onion or Japanese long onion (*naganegi*)

1 Tbsp vegetable oil

Teriyaki sauce (mixed in advance):

  2 Tbsp sugar

  ¼ cup (60 ml) soy sauce

  1 cup (240 ml) *sake*

½ tsp crushed chili pepper or *shichimi* spice powder (optional)

1   Cut the chicken into 1 ¼ in. (3 cm) cubes. Cut the bell pepper, mushrooms, and onion into pieces about the same size as the chicken. Thread the chicken, bell peppers, mushrooms, and onion onto skewers.

2   Heat the oil in a large frying pan over medium-low heat. Lay the skewers into the pan and cook for about 15 minutes, turning from time to time, until the chicken is nicely browned.

3   Add the teriyaki sauce to the pan and simmer, occasionally basting the skewers, until the sauce thickens and glazes the meat and vegetables, about 4 minutes.

4   Arrange the skewers on a serving platter and pour the sauce over. Serve with the crushed chili pepper and/or shichimi spice powder, if desired.

SAUTÉED PORK WITH GINGER AND TOMATO

SERVES TWO

INGREDIENTS

Thin-cut boneless pork loin chops, preferably from the shoulder end, about 7 oz. (200 g) total

2 Tbsp cornstarch

2 tsp vegetable oil

Teriyaki sauce (mixed in advance):

  1 ½ Tbsp sugar

  3 Tbsp soy sauce

  ¼ cup plus 2 Tbsp (90 ml) *sake*

½ regular tomato, cored and chopped

1 small knob ginger, peeled and grated

⅛ head cabbage, washed, very thinly shredded, and soaked in cold water

The rich aroma of soy sauce, sugar, and ginger from this dish is sure to whet your appetite.

1 Dust the pork with cornstarch. Place a frying pan over medium-high heat, add the oil, and sear the pork on both sides until golden brown.

2 Lower the heat to medium. Add the teriyaki sauce and simmer, shaking the pan from time to time, until the sauce thickens a little, about 4 minutes. Add the tomato, bring to a simmer again, and remove from heat. Add the grated ginger and its juice.

3 Arrange the pork on a serving plate with the sauce from the pan. Drain the cabbage and serve a generous heap of it on the side.

■ For the pork, thinner is better, so ask your butcher to cut the pork loin into ¼ in. (6 mm) or thinner chops.

■ The shredded cabbage is refreshing and offsets the richness of the pork. No dressing is needed!

SALMON TERIYAKI

INGREDIENTS

2 slices salmon, each 6 oz. (170 g)

Teriyaki sauce (mixed in advance):
- 2 ½ Tbsp sugar
- 3 Tbsp soy sauce
- ¼ cup plus 2 Tbsp (90 ml) *sake*

2 Tbsp cornstarch

1 Tbsp vegetable oil

1 tsp butter

Slivered lemon peel

The smokiness of the browned skin adds an appetizing aroma to this dish.

1 Marinate the salmon in the teriyaki sauce for about 10 minutes. Remove the salmon from the marinade, blot dry, and dust with the cornstarch. Reserve the teriyaki sauce.

2 Heat the oil in a frying pan over low heat. Sauté the salmon, skin-side down, until well-browned, fragrant and crisp. Turn over and cook until the flesh side is lightly browned. Remove from heat and take off the skin. Set aside.

3 In a separate pan, heat the butter until it foams. Pour in the reserved teriyaki sauce and simmer over low heat until the sauce thickens into a glaze. Add the salmon to the pan and baste with the sauce.

4 Pour the sauce into a serving dish. Arrange the salmon on the sauce and top with the slivered lemon peel.

ROLLED OMELET

INGREDIENTS

3 eggs

2 tsp chicken broth

3 Tbsp water

2 tsp soy sauce

1 Tbsp vegetable oil

1 in. (2.5 cm) length *daikon* radish, grated
  (about 2 Tbsp)

Soy sauce for grated daikon

■ Using a bamboo sushi mat and foil
sheets makes for a nicer cylinder,
but it's fine to use only a foil sheet
for rolling the omelet.

■ To make a sweeter style of rolled
omelet, add about two tablespoons
of sugar when beating the eggs.

This popular Japanese omelet is rolled into a flat
cylinder, allowed to cool, and sliced so that it is easy
to eat with chopsticks.

1 Lay a sheet of aluminum foil (about 12 in. / 30 cm square) on
a flat working surface such as a cutting board and poke tiny
holes here and there in the foil with a toothpick. Set aside.

2 Beat the eggs vigorously in a bowl and add the chicken broth,
water and soy sauce. Heat the vegetable oil in a frying pan
over medium-low heat and pour in the egg mixture. As soon as
the eggs start to set, begin to stir slowly and constantly with a
rubber spatula or a wooden spoon. Cook until fully set but still
moist.

3 Spread the eggs in the center of the aluminum foil and wrap
the foil around them securely. Press lightly to form a cylinder
and allow to cool to room temperature.

4 When cool, unwrap, cut the roll into pieces 1 in. (2.5 cm) thick,
and arrange on a serving plate. Mound the grated daikon radish on the side and drizzle a little soy sauce on the daikon.
Serve at room temperature.

Spread the eggs in the center of the foil
and begin to roll.

Roll the eggs securely. Tuck in both
ends if the eggs come out.

Allow to cool to room temperature to
set the rolled omelet.

GRILLED EGGPLANT IN SAUCE

INGREDIENTS

4 small eggplants

Sauce:

- 2 Tbsp soy sauce
- 1 Tbsp sugar
- 2 tsp chicken broth
- 2 Tbsp water

1 small knob ginger, peeled and grated

2 pinches dried bonito flakes (optional)

If possible, select smaller, sweeter eggplants (often sold as "Italian eggplants") for this dish.

1 Fill a large bowl with ice water. Lightly poke holes in the eggplants with a fork. Spear each eggplant on a long fork and grill directly over a gas flame until the entire surface is scorched. Plunge the eggplants in the ice water for a few seconds, then take them out and peel them, leaving the hard stem attached.

2 Mix the sauce ingredients in a small bowl.

3 Arrange the eggplants on a serving plate and pour the sauce over. Serve at room temperature, topped with grated ginger and bonito flakes, if desired.

Turn the eggplants constantly over a flame until they are charred.

Shock in ice water for few seconds to stop cooking.

Gently peel off the blackened skins. You can use a paper towel to peel.

CHAPTER 3

Deep-Fried Dishes

【*Agemono*】

Deep-frying cooks food quickly from all sides, almost like high-temperature steaming, maximizing sweetness and savor. When deep-frying at home, try to work in small batches. Chose a medium-sized (3 to 4 quart / liter) pot and use enough oil to fill the pan 2 in. (5 cm) deep. Transferring fried foods onto a wire rack to drain oil and release steam makes them crispier and healthier.

SHRIMP TEMPURA

INGREDIENTS

Tempura batter:

- 1 egg
- ¾ cup (180 ml) cold water
- 1 cup (125 g) flour

6 uncooked shrimp, thawed and patted dry if frozen

½ cup (60 g) flour for dusting shrimp

Vegetable oil for deep-frying

Set aside ½ tsp salt for each serving, or use tempura dipping sauce (see page 104)

It's easy to make great shrimp tempura at home. For frying the tempura, the oil should be at least 2 in. (5 cm) deep.

1 Beat the egg in a medium bowl and add the cold water and 1 cup flour. Lightly stir with a whisk or chopsticks until almost combined, but with some lumps remaining. Cover the bowl with plastic wrap and refrigerate.

2 Remove the shells from the shrimp but leave the tails attached. Cut off the stiff spike at the tail, if attached. Devein the shrimp. Make a few shallow cuts in the belly side, cutting halfway through the shrimp at ½ in. (1 cm) intervals, to prevent them from curling up while frying.

3 Begin heating the vegetable oil to 355° F (180° C) in a medium-sized heavy pot.

4 Dust the shrimp with flour and pat off any excess. Remove the chilled batter from the refrigerator. Holding the shrimp by its tail, dip it into the batter, then slip it into the oil headfirst and deep-fry for 2 minutes until the batter is crisp. Transfer onto a wire rack.

5 Arrange the shrimp on a platter, preferably on absorbent paper to maintain crispness. Mound ½ tsp salt on individual serving dishes, or serve with tempura dipping sauce in individual bowls.

Cut off the spike above the tail (if attached) to keep the hot oil from spattering when deep-frying.

Dusting the shrimp with flour allows the batter to cling more easily.

When deep-frying, slip the shrimp into the oil headfirst.

■ Vegetable tempura (bell peppers, *kabocha*, onion, lotus root, etc.) is made in the same fashion as shrimp—by dusting ingredients with flour, dipping in cold batter, and deep-frying. Vegetables should be sliced about ½ in. thick. If frying *shiso* or basil leaves, batter only one side and fry at a lower temperature—about 320 °F (160 °C).

KAKIAGE TEMPURA

INGREDIENTS

1 oz. (30 g) carrot

1 oz. (30 g) *kabocha* squash, or other winter squash

1 oz. (30 g) burdock root or parsnip

4 sprigs chervil, cut into 2 in. (5 cm) lengths

Tempura batter:

- 3 Tbsp flour
- 2 Tbsp cold water

Vegetable oil for deep-frying

Tempura dipping sauce (see page 104)

The vegetables in *kakiage* are deep-fried in one piece to create a combination of flavors.

1 Peel the carrot and squash and cut into thin sticks about 2 in. (5 cm) long. Wash the burdock root in water with a stiff brush, and shred with a vegetable peeler.

2 Begin heating the vegetable oil to 355°F (180°C) in a medium-sized heavy pot.

3 Place the carrot, squash, burdock root, chervil, flour and water in a bowl and lightly mix to bind the vegetables together. The batter should be rather runny with some lumps remaining. Place half of the vegetable-batter mixture on a flat spatula and slowly slip it into the oil near the side of the pot, rather than the middle. Deep-fry for 2 minutes, until the batter is crisp. Transfer onto a wire rack. Repeat with remaining mixture.

4 Serve with tempura dipping sauce.

The shredded vegetables tend to scatter in the oil. To bind them together neatly, use a flat spatula such as a turner or fish spatula.

DEEP-FRIED OYSTERS

INGREDIENTS

10 fresh oysters, shelled

1 qt. (1 L) salt water (combine 1 qt. /
    1 L cold water with 2 Tbsp salt)

Salt to taste

Ground black pepper to taste

¼ cup (30 g) flour

2 eggs, beaten

1 cup (45 g) *panko* or other bread crumbs

Worcestershire sauce or wasabi-mayo
    sauce (see page 105)

2 leaves green-leaf lettuce

2 lemon wedges

Fried oysters are delicious with Worcestershire sauce or with homemade *wasabi*-mayo sauce—it depends on your personal preference.

1 Rinse the oysters well in the salt water, drain, and pat dry. Sprinkle with salt and black pepper. Place flour, beaten egg, and panko bread crumbs in separate bowls. Dust the oysters with flour and shake off any excess, then dip them in the beaten egg and coat evenly. Roll the oysters in bread crumbs and coat thoroughly, pressing the bread crumbs in by hand.

2 Heat the vegetable oil to 355 °F (180 °C) in a medium-sized heavy pot. Deep-fry the oysters for 3 to 4 minutes until the bread crumbs are golden brown.

3 Arrange the lettuce on a serving plate and top with the oysters and lemon wedges. Drizzle with Worcestershire sauce or serve with wasabi-mayo sauce.

JAPANESE PORK CUTLETS

INGREDIENTS

2 boneless pork chops, about
    4 oz. (120 g) each

Salt to taste

Ground black pepper to taste

$\frac{1}{4}$ cup (30 g) flour

2 eggs, beaten

1 cup (45 g) panko or other bread crumbs

Vegetable oil for deep-frying

Worcestershire sauce or soy-sesame
    sauce (see page 105)

Vegetable garnishes (see sidebar)

In this dish, Japanese pork cutlets, about $\frac{1}{2}$ in. (1$\frac{1}{4}$ cm) thick, are deep-fried with coarse *panko* bread crumbs. Many supermarkets have started to sell panko, but if you can't find it, any white bread crumbs can be used.

1 Season the pork chops on both sides with salt and pepper. Place flour, beaten egg, and bread crumbs in separate bowls. Dust the pork chops with flour, then dip in the beaten egg and coat evenly. Roll in bread crumbs and coat thoroughly, pressing the bread crumbs into the pork chops by hand.

2 Heat the vegetable oil to 355°F (180°C) in a medium-sized heavy pot. Deep-fry the pork chops until the bread crumbs turn golden brown. Transfer to a wire rack.

3 Cut the cutlets into 1 in. (2.5 cm) thick slices. Arrange the cutlets on a serving plate along with the vegetable garnishes. Drizzle with Worcestershire sauce or soy-sesame sauce.

■ Pork cutlets go well with any vegetable. Shredded cabbage is the classic accompaniment, but I use pieces of carrot and kabocha squash cooked in the microwave for 2 to 3 minutes and arranged on the side with parsley.

DEEP-FRIED MARINATED CHICKEN BREAST

INGREDIENTS

11 oz. (310 g) chicken breast, cut into bite-sized pieces

1 egg yolk

1 Tbsp soy sauce

2 tsp sake

2 tsp grated ginger

2 Tbsp flour

Vegetable oil for deep-frying

½ cup (60 g) cornstarch

2 lemon wedges

Chicken breast often turns out dry when cooked, but marinating it in *sake*, soy sauce, and ginger keeps it moist and flavorful.

1 Beat the egg yolk in a medium bowl, add the soy sauce, sake, grated ginger and flour, and mix until just combined. Coat the chicken and leave for 20 minutes.

2 Heat the vegetable oil to 355°F (180°C) in a medium-sized heavy pot. Dust the chicken in the cornstarch and shake off any excess. Deep-fry the chicken in the oil until the coating becomes crisp, 5 to 6 minutes. Transfer onto a wire rack.

3 Arrange on a serving platter, preferably on absorbent paper, and put the lemon wedges on the side.

DEEP-FRIED COD

SERVES TWO

INGREDIENTS

3 ½ oz. (200 g) cod fillets

2 Tbsp soy sauce

1 Tbsp *sake*

Salad:

- 2 tender leaves green-leaf lettuce, washed and dried
- ½ small red bell pepper, seeded and thinly sliced
- ½ small yellow bell pepper, seeded and thinly sliced

Vegetable oil for deep-frying

½ cup (60 g) cornstarch

1 tsp lemon peel, minced

1 tsp parsley leaves, minced

A comforting yet appetizing dish full of fragrance, with soy sauce, lemon peel, and parsley.

1 Remove the skin and pin bones from the cod and cut into large pieces. Combine the soy sauce and sake in a bowl, coat the cod thoroughly, and leave for 15 minutes.

2 To make the salad, tear the lettuce into pieces. Combine the lettuce and bell peppers and refrigerate.

3 Heat the vegetable oil to 355 °F (180 °C) in a medium-sized heavy pot. Add the cornstarch, lemon peel, and parsley leaves directly to the bowl in which the cod is marinating and mix to coat the cod thoroughly. Deep-fry in the oil until the batter is lightly browned, 3 to 4 minutes. Transfer onto a wire rack. Arrange the salad in a serving bowl and serve the cod on top.

DEEP-FRIED TOFU

INGREDIENTS

Broth:

- 1 Tbsp chicken broth
- 4 Tbsp water
- 2 tsp soy sauce
- 2 tsp sugar

½ block firm tofu (about 6 oz. / 170 g), cut in two

1 Tbsp cornstarch

Vegetable oil for deep-frying

1 in. (2.5 cm) length *daikon* radish, grated (about 2 Tbsp total)

½ tsp ground or crushed chili pepper

1 large knob ginger, peeled and grated

1 scallion, finely chopped

This is another great tofu dish. Mixing the grated radish, ginger, and scallions into the broth makes a refreshing sauce that lightens the fried tofu.

1 Combine the chicken broth, water, soy sauce and sugar in a small saucepan and heat to dissolve the sugar. Set aside. Begin heating the vegetable oil to 355 °F (180 °C) in a medium-sized heavy pot.

2 Dust the tofu with cornstarch, brushing off any excess. Place a piece of tofu on a wire skimmer or slotted spoon and plunge in the oil. Deep-fry until the surface becomes golden brown, about 6 minutes, and transfer onto a wire rack. Repeat with the other piece of tofu.

3 Place the fried tofu in a serving bowl and pour in the broth. Mix the grated daikon radish and ground chili pepper together and mound on the tofu, followed by the grated ginger and chopped scallion. Just before eating, mix the grated daikon, ginger and scallions into the broth.

Pat off any excess cornstarch from the tofu.

Tofu can be deep-fried by submerging it halfway in the oil in a heavy-duty frying pan.

CHICKEN WINGS ESCABECHE

INGREDIENTS

Vegetable oil for deep-frying

6 large chicken wings

½ cup (60 g) flour

Marinade:

- ½ cup (120 ml) white or red wine vinegar
- ⅓ cup (80 ml) chicken broth
- 1⅓ cup (320 ml) water
- 3 Tbsp soy sauce
- 3 Tbsp sugar
- ½ tsp crushed chili pepper

½ onion, peeled and shredded

¼ carrot, peeled and shredded

1 tsp minced lemon peel

2 scallions, cut into thin slices

2 tsp toasted sesame seeds

Marinating the chicken wings after frying makes them light and refreshing. You can keep the wings refrigerated in the marinade for up to 3 days.

1 Heat the vegetable oil to 355°F (180°C) in a medium-sized heavy pot. Dust the chicken with the flour and deep-fry in the oil until the surface is golden brown, about 5 to 6 minutes. Transfer onto a wire rack.

2 Combine all marinade ingredients in a saucepan and bring to a simmer. Add the fried chicken wings, onion, and carrot, stir once and turn off the heat. Allow to cool to room temperature.

3 Arrange the chicken in a shallow serving bowl and top with the onion and carrot. Sprinkle with the lemon peel, scallions, and sesame seeds.

CHAPTER 4

Steamed Dishes

【*Mushimono*】

Steaming cooks foods gently
and evenly—the perfect method
for delicate fish, eggs, and
vegetables. You don't need a
steamer to make these dishes;
you can use the stovetop, the
oven, or even the microwave.

SAKE-STEAMED CLAMS

INGREDIENTS

14 oz. (400 g) unshelled steamer clams

1 qt. (1 L) water

2 Tbsp salt

½ cup (120 ml) sake

½ cup (120 ml) water

1 tsp soy sauce

Juice squeezed from 2 large knobs
    peeled, grated ginger (about 2 tsp)

1 to 2 scallions, chopped

Steaming in *sake* is the best way to enjoy the delicate sweetness of fresh clams.

1 Rinse the clams in running cold water and place in a bowl. Mix the 1 qt. (1 L) water and 2 Tbsp salt and pour over the clams to barely cover. Cover and let stand for 20 minutes so that the clams expel all their sand, then rinse the clams in cold water.

2 Place the clams, sake, ½ cup water, and soy sauce in a single layer in a pan and bring to a simmer. Cover with a lid and cook the clams until they open, for 5 to 10 minutes. Discard any unopened clams.

3 Arrange the clams and cooking liquid in a serving bowl and sprinkle with the ginger juice and chopped scallions.

STEAMED VEGETABLES WITH PEANUT BUTTER DRESSING

SERVES TWO

INGREDIENTS

Peanut butter dressing:

- 3 Tbsp salted peanut butter
- 3 Tbsp soy sauce
- 1 ½ Tbsp white wine vinegar
- 1 ½ Tbsp sugar
- 1 Tbsp crushed peanuts

1 medium all-purpose potato, peeled

½ medium carrot, peeled

3 ½ oz. (100 g) *kabocha* squash or other winter squash

10 green beans, trimmed and cut into 2 in. (5 cm) lengths

3 Tbsp water

For this dish the vegetables are steamed in the microwave, a great method for retaining flavor and nutrients.

1   Combine all peanut butter dressing ingredients in a small bowl.

2   Cut the potato, carrot, and squash into thin sticks, 2 in. (5 cm) long. Place the vegetables in a heat-proof bowl and sprinkle with the water. Cover with plastic wrap and microwave until tender, about 2 minutes. Unwrap and drain on paper towels or in a sieve.

3   Arrange the vegetables in a serving bowl with extra dressing on the side.

■ Zucchini, asparagus, broccoli, and cauliflower are also good for steaming.

STEAMED EGG CUSTARD

INGREDIENTS

Two oven-proof cups or small bowls, each able to hold 1 cup (16 oz. / 240 ml) liquid

An oven-proof pan with a rim about 1 ½ in. (3 to 4 cm) high, large enough to hold both custard cups

Egg mixture:

- 2 large eggs
- ⅓ cup (80 ml) chicken broth
- 1 ⅓ cups (320 ml) water
- 2 tsp soy sauce

2 fresh shiitake mushrooms, cleaned and stems trimmed

2 medium shrimp, shelled and deveined

1 ½ oz. (40 to 50 g) chicken breast, without skin, halved

Leaves from 2 sprigs chervil or *mitsuba* herb

Slivered lemon peel

Hot water

2 pinches ground chili pepper

As the eggs set into a savory custard, they absorb and hold the succulent juices from the chicken, *shiitake* mushrooms, and shrimp. Serve as a hot appetizer.

1 Preheat the oven to 355° F (180° C).

2 Crack the eggs into a bowl and mix gently so as not to create bubbles. Add the chicken broth, water, and soy sauce, and strain through a fine-mesh sieve to make a smooth mixture.

3 Divide the mushrooms, shrimp, chicken, and chervil leaves between the cups and pour equal amounts of egg mixture into each. Top with lemon peel and cover each cup with foil. Put the cups in a pan with a high rim and add enough hot water to come ½ in. (1 cm) up the sides of the cups. Transfer the pan to the oven and bake for 30 minutes. When done (see sidebar) remove from the oven and allow to cool slightly.

4 When cool enough to handle, unwrap and serve. Top with ground chili pepper if desired.

■ To check doneness, remove a cup from the oven, unwrap, and use a bamboo skewer or toothpick to poke a hole in the custard all the way to the bottom of the cup. If clear liquid wells up out of the hole, the custard is done. If the liquid is cloudy, return to the oven for another 5 minutes, then check again.

Strain the egg mixture through a fine-mesh sieve.

Oven-steaming is simple and easy if you have a pan with a high rim.

STEAMED SALMON WITH TOFU AND MUSHROOMS

INGREDIENTS

2 pieces dried kombu kelp, each about 2 in. (5 cm) square

2/3 cup (160 ml) *sake*

2/3 cup (160 ml) water

1 1/2 Tbsp soy sauce

2 salmon fillets or steaks, about 4 oz. (120 g) each

Salt to taste

Ground black pepper to taste

1/2 block tofu, about 6 oz. (170 g)

4 oz. (120 g) mushrooms, such as *shiitake*, *maitake*, *enoki*, or regular button mushrooms

Juice of 1/2 lemon

Slivered lemon peel (optional)

6 snow peas, trimmed and blanched in boiling water (optional)

The *kombu* need not be eaten—it may be a bit tough—but its *umami* surely enhances this dish.

1 Combine the kombu, sake and water in a bowl and leave overnight. Remove the kombu and add the soy sauce to the liquid.

2 Sprinkle the salmon slices with salt and pepper on both sides. Cut the tofu in half. Wipe the mushrooms clean, trim hard parts off the stems, and cut or tear into bite-sized pieces.

3 Lay a piece of kombu in a heat-proof, shallow bowl suitable for one serving. Place half the mushrooms, tofu and salmon on the kombu and pour in half the sake-soy sauce mixture. Repeat in a separate bowl with the remaining ingredients. Cover each dish with plastic wrap and microwave for 4 to 5 minutes.

4 To serve, unwrap and sprinkle with the lemon juice. Top with the slivered lemon peel and blanched snow peas, if using.

CHAPTER **5**

Simmered Dishes

【*Nimono*】

Simmering meats, fish and
vegetables with just enough heat
makes them tender and succulent.
The dishes in this section are
cooked without a lid, but they
can be partially covered if the
ingredients begin to dry out on top.

BRAISED BEEF AND POTATOES

SERVES TWO

Beef and potatoes cooked in sweetened soy sauce is a ubiquitous home-cooked dish in Japan that just about everyone loves.

INGREDIENTS

4 oz. (120 g) ground beef

2 large potatoes (waxy type if available, rather than baking type)

1 Tbsp vegetable oil

$\frac{1}{3}$ cup (45 g) shelled or frozen green peas

1 cup (240 ml) water

2 Tbsp (240 ml) soy sauce

1 Tbsp sugar

2 scallions, thinly sliced

1 Wash the potatoes, peel, and cut into bite-sized pieces.

2 Heat the vegetable oil in a medium-sized saucepan. Add the beef and stir until it changes color. Add the potatoes, water, soy sauce, and sugar, and bring to a simmer over medium-high heat. Lower the heat and simmer uncovered until the potatoes are tender, about 20 minutes. Add the green peas and simmer until the liquid is almost gone.

3 Arrange the beef and potatoes in a serving bowl and top with the sliced scallions.

SIMMERED NAPA CABBAGE AND PORK SLICES

SERVES TWO

INGREDIENTS

½ head napa cabbage, about 2 ¼ lbs.
  (1 kg)

7 oz. (200 g) sliced fresh pork belly or
  bacon, cut into 2 in. (5 cm) pieces

1 ¼ cups (300 ml) water

2 Tbsp soy sauce

1 Tbsp sugar

Ground black pepper

Slivered lemon peel (optional)

The meltingly tender texture and sweet flavor of napa cabbage make it a popular vegetable for stews in Japan.

1 Cut off the base of the cabbage, wash the leaves, and cut them across the grain into 2 in. (5 cm) pieces.

2 Place the water, soy sauce, sugar, and pork belly or bacon in a medium-sized pot and bring to a simmer. Add the cabbage. When the liquid returns to a boil, lower the heat and cook uncovered at a gentle simmer until the cabbage is tender, about 15 minutes.

3 To serve, dust with ground black pepper and top with slivered lemon peel if desired.

■ If you can, ask your butcher for fresh pork belly sliced paper-thin. Fresh pork belly makes a clearer-tasting broth than bacon.

KABOCHA SQUASH AND BACON STEW

INGREDIENTS

7 oz. (200 g) kabocha squash

3 ½ oz. (100 g) sliced bacon (3 to 4 regular slices), chopped

1 cup (240 ml) water

1 Tbsp soy sauce

½ Tbsp sugar

1 to 2 sprigs parsley, chopped

Kabocha squash is worth seeking out for its sweet, buttery flavor, but any hard-shell squash can be substituted.

1   If using a whole squash, cut in half and remove the seeds and stringy pulp with a spoon. Cut each half into wedges, then cut into 2 in. (5 cm) pieces until you have about 7 oz. (200 g) total. Use a sharp knife to peel off the dark green rind off in places. Place the squash in a heat-proof dish, cover with plastic wrap, and microwave for 3 minutes.

2   Place the squash, chopped bacon, water, soy sauce, and sugar in a saucepan over medium-high heat and bring to a simmer. Lower the heat and simmer uncovered until the liquid is almost gone, about 10 minutes.

3   Arrange the squash and bacon in a serving bowl and sprinkle with chopped parsley.

If you have any leftovers, this dish tastes even better reheated the next day.

SWEET-AND-SOUR CHICKEN WINGS

INGREDIENTS

6 large chicken wings

1 tsp vegetable oil

½ cup (120 ml) white wine vinegar

½ cup (120 ml) water

2 Tbsp soy sauce

1 Tbsp sugar

6 thinly sliced lemon rounds

1 to 2 sprigs parsley, chopped

The refreshing aroma of vinegar and lemon makes this simmered chicken dish perfect for summer. It's good hot, warm, or cold.

1 Heat the vegetable oil in a frying pan and sear the chicken on both sides until lightly browned.

2 Place the seared chicken, white wine vinegar, water, soy sauce, and sugar in a medium-sized pot and bring to a simmer. Lower the heat and cook at a gentle simmer until the liquid is reduced but enough remains to cook the lemon slices. Add the lemon and continue to cook until the remaining liquid is almost gone.

3 Place the chicken and lemon in a serving bowl and sprinkle with the chopped parsley.

SIMMERED CALAMARI AND *DAIKON* RADISH

INGREDIENTS

3 in. (7.5 cm) length daikon radish, about 10 oz. (300 g), peeled and cut into bite-sized pieces

4 green beans, tops and tails removed

7 oz. (200 g) calamari, thawed if frozen

1 cup (240 ml) water

1 Tbsp plus 1 tsp soy sauce

1 Tbsp sugar

Pinch crushed chili pepper (or *shichimi* spice powder)

Calamari makes a surprisingly fragrant, deep-flavored broth, which is absorbed beautifully by the *daikon* radish in this dish.

1 Place the daikon radish in a heat-proof dish, cover with plastic wrap, and microwave for 5 minutes. Cut the green beans into 1 in. (2.5 cm) pieces.

2 Place the daikon, calamari, water, soy sauce and sugar in a medium-sized pot and bring to a simmer. Lower the heat and simmer uncovered until ¾ of the liquid is gone. Add the green beans and cook until they are tender.

3 To serve, sprinkle with crushed chili pepper.

GINGER MACKEREL

INGREDIENTS

2 cups (480 ml) water for blanching mackerel

2 mackerel fillets, preferably skin-on, each about 4 oz. (120 g)

1 knob ginger, peeled and thinly sliced

¾ cup (180 ml) water

¾ cup (180 ml) *sake*

¼ cup (60 ml) soy sauce

2 Tbsp sugar

Blanching fish with a strong taste like mackerel in boiling water removes much of the "fishy" flavor.

1 Bring water to a boil in a small saucepan. Have ice water ready in a medium bowl. Blanch one fillet for 10 seconds and immediately plunge it into the ice water. Repeat with the other fillet. Pat the mackerel dry with paper towels.

2 Place the mackerel in a saucepan and add the ¾ cup (180 ml) water, sake, soy sauce, and sugar. Bring to a simmer over medium-high heat. Add the ginger, lower the heat, and cook uncovered at a gentle simmer until the liquid is almost gone, about 10 minutes.

Using a slotted spoon, plunge the mackerel slice in boiling water.

Shock the mackerel slice in ice water, then pat dry with paper towels.

KIMPIRA

INGREDIENTS

9 in. (22 cm) length burdock root, about
   3 $\frac{1}{2}$ oz. (100 g)

$\frac{1}{3}$ medium carrot, peeled and cut into
   thin sticks

$\frac{1}{2}$ tsp crushed chili pepper or $\frac{1}{2}$ dried
   hot chili pepper sliced into thin rounds

2 tsp vegetable oil

2 tsp soy sauce

$\frac{1}{2}$ Tbsp sugar

1 tsp toasted sesame seeds

Kimpira, a classic dish on Japanese home tables, features burdock root and carrot cooked with soy sauce, sugar, and hot chili pepper.

1 Scrub the burdock root in cold water with a stiff brush (peeling is not necessary), and use a vegetable peeler to shave it into thin shreds.

2 Heat the vegetable oil in a frying pan or saucepan over medium-high heat, then add the burdock root, carrot, and chili pepper. Cook until the burdock root and carrot shed their juices and become slightly soft. Add the sugar and soy sauce and cook, stirring continuously, until the liquid is almost gone. Take care not to scorch the soy sauce.

3 Sprinkle with the sesame seeds before seving.

POTATO *KIMPIRA* WITH BACON

SERVES TWO

INGREDIENTS

2 medium all-purpose potatoes

2 slices bacon

1 Tbsp vegetable oil

½ tsp crushed chili pepper

1 Tbsp soy sauce

1 Tbsp sugar

1 Tbsp water

½ tsp toasted sesame seeds

1 scallion, chopped

Ground black pepper

For this dish potatoes are cut into sticks and sautéed with bacon until tender but still slightly crunchy. Parsnips are also good cooked this way.

1 Wash and peel the potatoes. Cut lengthwise into ¼ in. (7 mm) slices, and cut each slice into ¼ in. (7 cm) sticks. Chop the bacon roughly.

2 Place the vegetable oil, bacon, and crushed chili pepper in a frying pan over medium heat and cook until the bacon fat renders out. Add the potato, soy sauce, sugar, and water, and cook until the liquid is almost gone. Turn off the heat, sprinkle with the sesame seeds, and stir once.

3 Arrange the potato kimpira in a serving bowl and top with the chopped scallions and ground black pepper.

CHICKEN AND VEGETABLE STEW

INGREDIENTS

5 1/2 oz. (160 g) chicken breast

1/2 medium carrot, peeled

2 in. (5 cm) length lotus root, about
1 oz. (30 g), peeled (optional)

2 large fresh *shiitake* mushrooms

6 snow peas, stems and strings removed

2 cups (480 ml) water

3 Tbsp soy sauce

1 1/2 Tbsp sugar

2 tsp vegetable oil

1 tsp toasted sesame seeds

The best part of this dish is not the chicken, but rather the nutritious root vegetables, which soak up the savory chicken and mushroom juices.

1 Cut the chicken, carrot, and lotus root (if using) into bite-sized pieces. Remove the stem of each mushroom and cut in half.

2 Place the vegetable oil in a saucepan over medium-high heat. Add the chicken, carrot, lotus root, and mushrooms and sauté for 2 to 3 minutes. Add the water, soy sauce, and sugar, and bring to a simmer, then lower the heat and continue to simmer until the liquid is reduced, but enough remains to cook the snow peas. Add the peas and cook until tender. The liquid should be almost gone.

3 Arrange all ingredients in a serving bowl and sprinkle with the toasted sesame seeds.

■ Other root vegetables such as parsnips, rutabaga, burdock root, or bamboo shoots can also be used if lotus root is not available.

CHAPTER **6**

Hot Pots

【*Nabemono*】

Japanese hot pots are comforting and warming in the winter, yet light enough to be enjoyed in the heat of summer as well. Hot pots allow couples or families to share the same simmering pot, a communal experience that brings people a little closer.

SUKIYAKI

I add tomatoes to sukiyaki for their fresh *umami* flavor. If you are not comfortable with raw egg, omit it.

INGREDIENTS

½ block firm tofu or grilled tofu (*yaki-tofu*), about 6 oz. (170 g)

1 onion, peeled, halved ,and thickly sliced

2 tomatoes, halved and thickly sliced

½ bunch fresh spinach, about 3 ½ oz. (100 g), cut into 2 in. (5 cm) lengths

2 large fresh *shiitake* mushrooms, cleaned and stems trimmed

1 Japanese long onion (*naganegi*), thinly sliced on the diagonal (optional)

1 pack (7 oz. / 200 g) *konnyaku* noodles (optional, also called *shirataki*)

7 oz. (200 g) top-quality beef, thinly sliced

Sukiyaki sauce:

½ cup (120 ml) soy sauce

¼ cup (50 g) sugar

1 cup (240 ml) water

2 eggs, for dipping

1 Cut the tofu into 8 pieces. Blanch and drain the konnyaku noodles (if using), and cut them into bite-sized pieces.

2 Arrange the beef, vegetables, and konnyaku noodles in a large pot. Combine all the sukiyaki sauce ingredients in a small bowl and pour over the beef and vegetables. Turn on the heat and bring to a simmer. (This can also be done directly on the table with a portable gas burner.)

3 Crack the eggs into individual bowls and beat. To eat, pick up pieces of cooked beef and vegetables with chopsticks, dip into the beaten egg, and eat.

■ If you can't find thinly sliced beef, ask your butcher to cut ribeye or strip loin steak into paper-thin slices.

SHABU-SHABU HOT POT

SERVES TWO

INGREDIENTS

Ponzu sauce:

- ¼ cup (60 ml) soy sauce
- 2 Tbsp lemon juice
- 2 Tbsp vinegar
- 1 Tbsp sugar

Peanut sauce:

- 1 Tbsp peanut butter
- 1 Tbsp soy sauce
- 1 Tbsp lemon juice
- 2 tsp sugar

7 oz. (200 g) top-quality beef, thinly sliced

½ block tofu, 6 oz. (170 g)

½ head iceberg lettuce

⅓ medium carrot

2 large fresh *shiitake* mushrooms

1 oz. (30 g) *enoki* mushrooms (optional)

1 cup (240 ml) chicken broth

2½ cups (600 ml) water

"*Shabu-shabu*" takes its name from the sound of the beef being swished through the hot pot. The vegetables may be cooked a bit longer, but the beef should stay in the broth only briefly.

1 Make the ponzu and peanut sauces ahead of time: combine the ingredients of each in separate bowls and set aside.

2 Cut the tofu into large chunks. Cut the lettuce into bite-sized pieces. Peel the carrot and cut into thin rounds. Trim the stems from the mushrooms. Arrange the beef, tofu, lettuce, carrot and mushrooms on a serving plate.

3 Set a portable gas burner on the dining table. Place a medium saucepan or shallow pot on the burner, pour in the chicken broth and water, and bring to a simmer. Add the ingredients, starting with those that take longer to cook such as carrots, and ending with the beef. Use chopsticks to take out vegetables and meat as they are cooked, dip them in either kind of sauce, and eat.

CHICKEN MEATBALL HOT POT

INGREDIENTS

Chicken meatballs:

- 11 oz. (310 g) ground chicken
- 1 scallion, finely chopped
- 1 small knob ginger, peeled and finely chopped
- ½ egg, beaten
- 1 Tbsp soy sauce
- 1 Tbsp potato starch or cornstarch

2 ½ cups (600 ml) water

2 Tbsp soy sauce

Pinch salt

⅛ napa cabbage, chopped

3 ½ oz. (100 g) spinach or garlic chives (also called *nira*), chopped

Crushed chili pepper (or *shichimi* spice powder)

The fragrance of ginger in the chicken meatballs and the napa cabbage makes for a warming soup that is just slightly exotic.

1 Combine all the chicken meatball ingredients in a large bowl.

2 Pour the water into a large pan and bring to a simmer over medium heat. When the water is simmering, scoop up heaping tablespoons of the chicken meatball mixture, form them into balls, and add to the pan, maintaining a simmer. Use all the meatball mixture. Simmer until the chicken meatballs are cooked through.

3 Season to taste with soy sauce and salt, then add the napa cabbage and spinach or garlic chives. Cover and cook until tender.

4 Arrange the chicken meatballs, vegetables, and soup in individual bowls. Top with crushed chili pepper.

SALMON AND *MISO* HOT POT

INGREDIENTS

7 oz. (200 g) fresh salmon, skin removed

¼ head cabbage

1 large all-purpose potato

4 green beans

2 large fresh *shiitake* mushrooms

1 oz. (30 g) *enoki* mushrooms (optional)

½ cup (120 ml) chicken broth

1 ½ cups (360 ml) water

2 Tbsp yellow miso

1 Tbsp butter

This is a nourishing family recipe with salmon, *miso*, potatoes and other vegetables. A pat of butter added at the last minute enhances the sweet *umami* of the salmon.

1 Cut the salmon into bite-sized pieces. Peel the potato, cut into ½ in. (1 cm) thick rounds, blanch and drain. Cut the cabbage and green beans into bite-sized pieces. Trim the stems from the mushrooms.

2 Pour the chicken broth and water into a large pan and mix in the miso. Add the salmon and vegetables to the pot, cover, and bring to a simmer. (This can also be done at the table with a portable gas burner.) When the salmon and vegetables are cooked, add the butter and let it melt halfway before serving the hot pot.

CHAPTER 7

Rice and Noodles

【*Gohan and Men*】

A bowl of rice or noodles can be a quick and easy meal for either lunch or dinner. For directions on washing and cooking white rice in a regular pot, see page 98.

MARINATED TUNA ON RICE

SERVES TWO

INGREDIENTS

3 cups hot cooked rice, about 1 lb. (450 g)

Marinade:

- 3 Tbsp soy sauce
- 3 Tbsp *sake*
- 1 ½ Tbsp sugar
- 1 ½ Tbsp *wasabi* paste

7 oz. (200 g) *sashimi*-grade tuna, as fresh as possible

2 in. (5 cm) length *daikon* radish

1 cup (33 g) trimmed radish sprouts or chopped scallions, lightly packed

Tuna marinated in soy sauce on a bowl of hot rice is a healthy and satisfying full meal. If you can't find radish sprouts, use alfalfa sprouts or chopped scallions.

1 To make the marinade, combine the soy sauce, sake, and sugar in a medium saucepan, bring to a simmer and remove from heat. When cooled, mix in the wasabi paste.

2 Cut the fresh tuna into slices and soak in the pan of marinade for 5 minutes. Meanwhile, peel and grate the daikon radish. Place in a sieve and allow to drain for 2 to 3 minutes.

3 Arrange the rice in individual bowls and top with the marinated tuna slices. Mix some marinade in with the grated daikon radish to make a loose sauce. Spoon the sauce over the rice and tuna. Garnish with the radish sprouts.

CHICKEN AND MUSHROOM RICE

INGREDIENTS

4 cups hot cooked rice, about 1 ⅓ lbs. (600 g)

1 cup plus 3 Tbsp (285 ml) water

3 Tbsp soy sauce

3 Tbsp sugar

6 oz. (170 g) chicken breast, cut into bite-sized pieces

6 oz. (170 g) fresh mushrooms, wiped, trimmed and cut into ¼ in. (5 mm) cubes

1 large knob ginger, peeled and grated

2 tsp toasted sesame seeds

1 scallion, chopped

Finely diced lemon peel

10 leaves bibb lettuce (optional)

Delicious and easy to make, this dish features chicken and mushrooms mixed into cooked white rice.

1 Combine the water, soy sauce, and sugar in a small pan and add the chicken and mushrooms. Bring to a simmer and cook until the liquid is almost gone. Turn off the heat and mix in the ginger, sesame seeds, scallions, and lemon peel.

2 Gently mix the rice and all the ingredients from step 1 in a large bowl. Arrange in individual bowls or on a serving plate lined with the bibb lettuce, if using.

■ Choose a few different kinds of mushrooms that are good for cooking and combine them. Here I used 2 large *shiitake*, 2 oz. (60 g) *maitake*, and 2 oz. (60 g) *shimeji* mushrooms.

SMOKED SALMON, BUTTER, AND SOY SAUCE ON RICE

SERVES TWO

INGREDIENTS

3 cups hot cooked rice, about 1 lb. (450 g)

6 ½ oz. (180 g) thinly sliced smoked salmon

2 pieces butter, each ½ Tbsp (7.5 g)

2 Tbsp soy sauce

¼ onion, thinly sliced

2 pinches radish sprouts (optional)

Curly parsley for topping

This is one of my favorites. It's especially great when you're hungry and want to prepare a meal as quickly as possible.

Arrange the hot rice in individual bowls, top with butter, and sprinkle with soy sauce. Place the onion slices and radish sprouts (if using) over half of the rice, then lay the smoked salmon slices on the other half. Top with curly parsley.

CHICKEN AND EGG ON RICE

INGREDIENTS

3 cups hot cooked rice, about 1 lb. (450 g)

1 Tbsp chicken broth

4 Tbsp water

2 Tbsp soy sauce

1 Tbsp plus 2 tsp sugar

7 oz. (200 g) chicken breast, cut into bite-sized pieces

½ onion, thinly sliced

6 eggs, beaten

2 scallions, chopped, for topping

Crushed chili pepper (or *shichimi* spice powder)

The egg thickens the seasoned chicken broth in this dish so that it clings to the rice, making a hot and comforting lunch.

1 Combine the chicken broth, water, soy sauce and sugar in a medium saucepan or frying pan. Add the chicken and onion and bring to a simmer over high heat. Simmer until the chicken is just cooked through. Pour in the beaten egg slowly, reduce the heat to low, and cook the egg to desired doneness by shaking the pan without stirring. (It's best if it's still a little runny.)

2 Arrange the rice in individual bowls and ladle the egg-and-chicken mixture over top. Garnish with chopped scallions and crushed chili pepper.

FRIED RICE

INGREDIENTS

4 cups hot cooked rice, about 1 ⅓ lbs. (600 g)

2 eggs, beaten

2 Tbsp vegetable oil

1 bunch scallions, chopped

1 small knob ginger, peeled and chopped

1 Tbsp soy sauce

½ cup (5 g) lightly packed dried bonito flakes (optional)

2 Tbsp toasted sesame seeds

1 Tbsp soy sauce for sprinkling

3 *shiso* leaves, minced, or a small bunch of cilantro leaves (optional)

My favorite fried rice is made with eggs, scallions, ginger, sesame seeds, and soy sauce. I mix the beaten eggs with the rice before frying so that the flavors mingle better.

1 Combine the cooked rice and beaten eggs in a bowl.

2 Heat the vegetable oil in a large frying pan or well-seasoned wok, add the scallions and ginger, and cook until the scallions are soft. Add the cooked rice and stir-fry until hot. Add the soy sauce and bonito flakes (if using), and stir-fry until the rice is dry and fluffy. To finish, sprinkle with sesame seeds and soy sauce, stir once and remove from heat.

3 Serve topped with the minced shiso leaves or cilantro (if using).

SUSHI RICE BOWL

INGREDIENTS

4 cups sushi rice, about 1 ⅓ lbs. (600 g)
(see page 100)

1 tsp toasted sesame seeds

1 small knob ginger, peeled and grated

2 tsp minced lemon peel

¼ small head iceberg lettuce, finely
chopped

2 tsp (or more) *wasabi* paste

Topping suggestions:

¼ small onion

½ avocado (and lemon juice for
sprinkling)

Rolled omelet (see page 28), made
from 1 egg

½ Japanese cucumber or ¼ peeled
and seeded English cucumber

1 ½ oz. (40 g) fresh tuna

1 ½ oz. (40 g) smoked salmon

2 large cooked shrimp

2 Tbsp *ikura* salmon roe

We serve this dish at home when celebrating a special occasion. You can add or omit any ingredients as you wish.

1 For the toppings, cut each ingredient except the onion into ½ in. (1 cm) cubes. Slice the onion very thinly. You may want to sprinkle lemon juice over the avocado to keep it from turning brown.

2 Combine the sushi rice with the toasted sesame seeds, ginger, lemon peel, lettuce, and wasabi in a large bowl. To mix, do not stir vigorously, but gently combine all ingredients by flipping the rice from the bottom to the top and cutting the seasonings into the rice with the edge of a flat spoon or paddle.

3 Place the seasoned rice in individual bowls and add your choice of toppings.

SUSHI HAND-ROLL WITH LETTUCE

INGREDIENTS

3 cups sushi rice, about 1 lb. (450 g) (see page 100)

8 hand-sized leaves green-leaf lettuce

Wasabi paste

Filling suggestions:

- Fresh or smoked salmon, *ikura* salmon roe, and sliced onion

- Scrambled eggs and flying-fish roe (*tobiko*)

- Cooked shrimp, avocado, and mayonnaise

- Marinated tuna (see page 72), toasted sesame seeds and scallions

When friends and family get together, everyone can enjoy assembling and rolling up sushi ingredients themselves and eating their creations. If you are familiar with *nori* seaweed, you can use it instead of lettuce.

Lay out the rice, lettuce leaves, wasabi paste, and fillings separately on a table. To eat, each person should make their own roll by putting some of the sushi rice on a lettuce leaf, smearing the rice with a little wasabi, and rolling it all up with the filling of their choice.

TUNA-MAYO RICE BALLS

MAKES EIGHT RICE BALLS

INGREDIENTS

A generous 3 cups hot cooked rice, about 17 oz. (480 g)

2 ½ oz. (70 g) canned tuna

2 heaping Tbsp mayonnaise

1 tsp soy sauce

1 scallion, chopped

3 Tbsp toasted sesame seeds

Canned tuna is common in Japanese pantries, and tuna and mayonnaise rice balls are as popular in Japan as tuna salad sandwiches are in the West.

1 Drain the canned tuna and break up in a bowl. Add the mayonnaise, soy sauce, and chopped scallion and mix.

2 Roughly divide the rice into eighths and place one eighth on an 8 in. (20 cm) sheet of plastic wrap. Flatten the rice a little and place one fourth of the tuna mixture in the center. Cover with another eighth of the rice, and use the plastic wrap to roll into a log shape around the filling. Repeat with the remaining ingredients to make 4 logs.

3 Spread the toasted sesame seeds on a shallow dish. Unwrap the rice logs and roll them in the sesame seeds. Cut each log in half and arrange on a serving dish. Serve with your favorite pickled vegetables on the side (I use thinly sliced *daikon* pickles).

Put a quarter of the tuna-mayo mixture in the center of the rice.

Roll the rice firmly into a log shape, but leave some air for a fluffier texture.

For this recipe, the sesame seeds should definitely be toasted for a richer flavor.

SEARED RICE BALLS WITH BACON SOY SAUCE

INGREDIENTS

A generous 3 cups hot cooked rice, about 17 oz. (480 g)

2 oz. (60 g) sliced bacon (about 2 regular slices), finely chopped

2 Tbsp soy sauce

4 Tbsp *sake*

1 Tbsp sugar

3 Tbsp minced lemon peel

1 Tbsp lemon juice

1 Tbsp toasted sesame seeds

1 tsp vegetable oil

Extra soy sauce for basting

These rice balls can be grilled or broiled. The mouth-watering scent of toasted rice and warm soy sauce makes them irresistible.

1 Combine the bacon, soy sauce, sake, and sugar in a small saucepan and reduce over low heat, stirring frequently until, the liquid is gone. Remove from heat and add the lemon peel, lemon juice, and toasted sesame seeds.

2 Spread ¼ of the rice on an 8 in. (20 cm) sheet of plastic wrap, and place ¼ of the bacon mixture in the center of the rice. Use the plastic wrap to shape the rice into a ball around the bacon, and then flatten slightly to form a thick patty. Repeat with the remaining portions.

3 In a non-stick frying pan, heat the vegetable oil over a medium flame. Unwrap the rice balls and sear until well browned on both sides, brushing with extra soy sauce after searing. Serve alongside your favorite pickled vegetables (here I used a pickled *umeboshi* plum).

Put a quarter of the bacon mixture in the center of the rice.

Shape the rice firmly into a ball, but leave some air for a fluffier texture.

Sear the rice balls to brown them slightly and brush with the soy sauce.

SOBA NOODLES WITH SWEET SOY SAUCE

INGREDIENTS

Sweet soy-sauce broth:

- ¼ cup (60 ml) chicken broth
- 1 cup (240 ml) water
- 2 Tbsp soy sauce
- 1 Tbsp sugar

1 scallion, chopped

8 oz. (230 g) dried soba buckwheat noodles

¼ onion (preferably a sweet variety), thinly sliced

½ cup (16 g) lightly packed trimmed sprouts, any kind

½ tsp prepared mustard (½ tsp each hot water and dry mustard powder, mixed well)

2 large pinches dried bonito flakes (optional)

Soba, traditional buckwheat noodles, are excellent served cold in a soy sauce-based broth with plenty of thinly sliced vegetables.

1 Combine the sweet soy-sauce broth ingredients in a small saucepan, bring to a simmer, and remove from heat. When cooled to room temperature, add the chopped scallion and set aside.

2 Bring a large pot of water to a boil. Add the soba noodles and cook according to the directions on the package. Drain the noodles and place immediately under cold running water to halt cooking. Drain very well and divide between individual bowls.

3 Arrange the sliced onion, sprouts, and a dab of mustard on top of the noodles in each bowl. Sprinkle with the dried bonito flakes, if using. Pour the broth over the noodles just before eating.

CHICKEN AND ONION NOODLE SOUP

SERVES TWO

INGREDIENTS

7 oz. (200 g) skinned chicken breast

1 tsp salt

1 bunch scallions, cut into 1 in. (2.5 cm) lengths

2 cups (480 ml) water

2 Tbsp soy sauce

1 tsp sugar

8 oz. (230 g) dried *soba* buckwheat noodles

Crushed chili pepper (or *shichimi* spice powder)

■ Whole-wheat pasta can be substituted for soba buckwheat noodles.

The best part of this soup is the scallions, so use the best, freshest green onions you can find.

1 Slice the chicken breast thinly at a steep angle to make wide slices. Sprinkle the salt on the slices and leave for 15 minutes.

2 Put the salted chicken and water in a medium saucepan and bring to a simmer. Add the soy sauce, sugar and scallions and simmer until the scallions are soft.

3 Meanwhile, bring a large pot of water to a boil. Add the noodles and cook according to the directions on the package. Drain very well and divide between individual bowls.

4 Ladle the chicken, scallions, and soup over top and garnish with crushed chili pepper.

FRIED NOODLES

INGREDIENTS

3 ½ oz. (100 g) *abura-age* deep-fried tofu, thawed if frozen

½ bunch scallions

8 oz. (230 g) dried *soba* buckwheat noodles

1 Tbsp vegetable oil

3 Tbsp soy sauce

2 Tbsp sake

1 tsp sugar

Crushed chili pepper (or *shichimi* spice powder)

½ cup (5 g) lightly packed dried bonito flakes (optional)

■ Whole-wheat pasta can be substituted for soba buckwheat noodles.

Frying noodles is a Chinese technique, but I like to add a Japanese touch by using buckwheat noodles, tofu, and *sake*.

1 Cut the deep-fried tofu into bite-sized pieces. Cut the scallions into 1 in. (2.5 cm) lengths.

2 Bring a large pot of water to a boil. Add the noodles and cook according to the directions on the package. Drain very well.

3 Heat the oil in a large frying pan over high heat. Once the oil shimmers, add the deep-fried tofu and scallions and cook until the scallions are slightly soft. Add the cooked noodles and stir-fry for a minute or two. Add the sake, soy sauce and sugar and stir-fry until the liquid has disappeared.

4 Serve the fried noodles on individual plates; garnish with crushed chili pepper and bonito flakes (if using).

BEEF NOODLE SOUP

INGREDIENTS

7 oz. (200 g) beef top round, thinly sliced

1 tsp salt

2 ½ cups (600 ml) water

3 Tbsp plus 1 tsp soy sauce

2 tsp sugar

1 bunch scallions, cut into 1 in. (2.5 cm) pieces

8 oz. (230 g) dried udon noodles

Crushed chili pepper (or *shichimi* spice powder)

Udon, thick wheat noodles, are now widely available in the West. If you can't find them, use any thick, substantial noodle.

1 Sprinkle the salt on the sliced beef and leave for 15 minutes.

2 Put the salted beef and water in a medium saucepan and bring to a simmer. Add the soy sauce, sugar and scallions and simmer until the scallions are soft.

3 Meanwhile, bring a large pot of water to a boil. Add the udon noodles and cook according to the directions on the package. Drain very well and divide between individual bowls. Ladle the beef, scallions, and soup over top and garnish with crushed chili pepper.

■ You can substitute soba buckwheat noodles or whole wheat pasta for udon noodles.

CHAPTER **8**

Soups

【*Wanmono*】

Soups are eaten throughout the course of the meal at the Japanese table, accompanying rice and other side dishes. Here are some simple yet hearty recipes that bring out the natural, wholesome flavors of their ingredients.

EGG AND BACON SOUP

INGREDIENTS

2 cups (480 ml) water

⅛ onion, sliced

2 oz. (60 g) sliced bacon (about 2 regular slices), cut into pieces

2 eggs

1 Tbsp cornstarch

2 tsp soy sauce

Pinch salt

1 tsp parsley, chopped

A hearty but delicate soup, with a pleasant smoky aroma from the bacon.

1 Combine the water, onion, and bacon in a small saucepan and bring to a simmer. Meanwhile, beat the eggs and combine with the cornstarch. When the water simmers, add the soy sauce and salt. Pour in the egg mixture, stirring, and keep at a gentle simmer until the eggs set.

2 Ladle into individual bowls and top with the chopped parsley.

CHICKEN AND TOFU SOUP

INGREDIENTS

6 oz. (170 g) boneless chicken thighs

1/3 block firm tofu, about 4 oz. (120 g)

1/3 medium carrot

4 in. (10 cm) stalk celery

2 Tbsp vegetable oil

2 cups (480 ml) water

Scant 1 tsp salt

1 Tbsp soy sauce

1/2 scallion, chopped

2 pinches crushed chili pepper (or *shichimi* spice powder)

This soup derives its *umami* from the chicken and tofu, so you don't need to add broth to give it flavor.

1 Cut the chicken thighs into 1/2 in. (1 cm) cubes. Break up the tofu into coarse pieces. Cut the carrot and celery into thin sticks.

2 Put the oil in a saucepan over medium heat. Add the chicken, tofu, carrot and celery and sauté until the surface of the chicken changes color. Pour in the water, bring to a simmer and cook until the vegetables are tender. Season with salt and soy sauce.

3 Ladle into individual bowls and top with the chopped scallions and crushed chili pepper.

CLAM AND *MISO* SOUP

INGREDIENTS

7 oz. (200 g) steamer clams, expelled of
  sand (see page 44)

2 cups (480 ml) water

2 Tbsp miso (any kind)

Pinch sugar

½ scallion, chopped

I like to use my favorite red *miso* made only with whole soybeans and salt for this soup, but try it with any kind of miso you can find.

1 Combine the clams and water in a small saucepan and bring to a simmer. Cook until the clams open, then turn off the heat and stir in the miso and sugar.

2 Ladle clams and soup into individual bowls and top with the chopped scallions. When eating, use fingers and/or chopsticks to remove the meat from the shells.

Scoop the miso with a ladle, dip into the broth, and stir in the miso little by little.

Do not allow the soup to boil after adding the miso or it will become sour and unpleasant.

PORK AND ROOT VEGETABLE SOUP

INGREDIENTS

3 ½ oz. (100 g) pork slices or cubes cut from loin, belly or ham

½ tsp salt

1 medium all-purpose potato

½ small onion

⅓ small carrot

2 tsp vegetable oil

1 ⅔ cups (400 ml) water

2 Tbsp miso, any kind

½ scallion, chopped

2 pinches ground red pepper

Rich with pork and *miso*, this is a great soup for a cold winter day.

1 Sprinkle the pork with the salt and leave for 15 minutes. Peel the potato, onion, and carrot and cut into small bite-sized pieces.

2 Heat the vegetable oil in a medium saucepan and add the carrot, potato, onion, and pork. Sauté until the pork is just cooked through. Pour in the water, bring to a simmer, and cook until the potato is tender. Stir in the miso. Do not allow the soup to boil after adding the miso.

3 Serve in individual bowls and top with the scallion and ground red pepper.

Supplemental Recipes

Rice

For Japanese cooking, use short-grain rice (sometimes labeled sushi rice). Short-grain rice and long-grain rice contain starches in different proportions. When cooked, short-grain rice becomes moist and cohesive, while remaining airy and light.

COOKED RICE

MAKES ABOUT 4¾ CUPS (880 G) COOKED RICE

The amount of water needed for cooking rice depends upon the humidity of the dry rice, the strength of the heat source, and the size and material of the cooking pot. Please note that following method and amounts are just a starting point. If the rice turns out too hard and dry, increase the water by a tablespoon and try again. If the rice turns out soggy or mushy, decrease the water by a tablespoon.

INGREDIENTS

2 cups (400 g) short-grain rice

2 cups plus 2 Tbsp water (510 ml)

1   Working in a sink, place the rice in a large bowl and add enough water to cover the rice by 1 in. (2.5 cm). Swish the rice around by hand for a few seconds; the water will become cloudy. Pour off the water immediately, placing one hand on the rice to keep it from spilling out of the bowl.

2   Pour in water just to cover the rice and swish by hand. When the water becomes cloudy, pour it off. Repeat three or four times. It's fine if the water is still a little cloudy.

3   Drain the rice in a sieve, then place in a medium saucepan with 2 cups plus 2 Tbsp water and allow to soak for 20 minutes.

4   Turn the heat to medium, cover, and bring to a boil. The water ideally should come to a boil in 5 to 10 minutes. Once it comes to a boil, immediately decrease the heat to very low and cook for 15 minutes.

5   Turn off the heat and leave undisturbed for 10 minutes. Uncover, and using a large spoon, bring the rice up from the bottom of the pot to the top, releasing steam and aerating the rice.

- A 2 qt. (2 L) saucepan is shown in these photos.
- Rice keeps for 3 days in the refrigerator, or longer in the freezer. Microwave or steam the rice to reheat.

VINEGARED SUSHI RICE

MAKES ABOUT 4¾ CUPS (880 G) COOKED RICE

Rice cooked for sushi should be slightly firmer in texture than regular cooked rice, so that it can absorb the seasoned vinegar added after cooking.

INGREDIENTS

Sushi vinegar:

- 3½ Tbsp rice vinegar
- 2½ Tbsp sugar
- 2 tsp salt

Just-cooked rice made from 2 cups (400 g) uncooked short-grain rice and 2 cups (480 ml) water (see directions on previous page)

1   While the rice is cooking, combine the rice vinegar, sugar, and salt in a non-reactive saucepan over medium-low heat. Stir constantly until the sugar and salt dissolve completely. Immediately turn off the heat.

2   Place the hot rice in a large bowl. Sprinkle with all of the sushi vinegar and mix with a flipping and cutting motion to evenly distribute the vinegar and aerate the rice.

Dashi

I use store-bought chicken broth throughout the book, diluting it with water to make the taste lighter (the proportion of chicken broth to water is written in each recipe). When using traditional dashi stock for a recipe, replace the total amount of chicken broth and water with *dashi*.

You can make a very good broth that works well for Japanese cuisine using ordinary tap water, chicken breast, and sun-dried tomatoes. You can also make a vegetarian/vegan broth with dried shiitake mushrooms and kombu seaweed.

EASY *DASHI*

MAKES ABOUT 1.8 QUARTS (1.8 L)

Here is a very quick and easy basic *dashi* stock recipe.

INGREDIENTS

2 pieces dried *kombu* kelp, each about 4 in. (10 cm) square

3 cups (30 g) lightly packed dried bonito flakes

2 qts. (2 L) water

1   Combine the kombu and water in a pot over medium-low heat. The water should be approaching a boil after about 20 minutes (adjust the heat if the water looks like it's coming to a boil too soon or too slowly). Once the water comes to a boil, immediately turn off the heat and remove the kombu with tongs.

2   Add the dried bonito flakes all at once. Wait until they absorb the water and sink.

3   Strain the broth through a fine-mesh sieve. For extra-clear dashi, line the strainer with two layers of cheesecloth.

■ Dashi is best used the same day it is made, but it may be kept in the refrigerator for up to 3 days. It can also be frozen.

EXTRA-RICH *DASHI*

MAKES ABOUT 1.8 QUARTS (1.8 L)

This professional method uses generous amounts of ingredients for more depth of flavor. You will need a thermometer, a kitchen scale, and fine-mesh cheesecloth or cotton gauze.

INGREDIENTS

1 oz. (30 g) dried *kombu* kelp

1¾ oz. (50 g) dried bonito flakes

2 qts. (2 L) water, preferably soft bottled water

1   Combine the kombu and water in a stock pot over high heat. When the water temperature reaches 140°F (60°C), lower the heat to maintain a constant water temperature of 140°F (60°C). Steep the kombu in the water for 1 hour to extract its full *umami* flavor. Remove the kombu from the pot.

2   Increase the heat and bring the water temperature up to 185°F (85°C). Turn off the heat, add the dried bonito flakes all at once, and wait until all the flakes sink to the bottom of the pot (you can push them into the water with chopsticks or a fork, but do not stir the dashi or it will become cloudy and strong-tasting).

3   Line a sieve with the cheese cloth and strain the dashi. Do not squeeze the bonito flakes in the cloth, but let them drain naturally for several minutes until no more dashi passes through the strainer.

■ Japanese water is softer (that is, lower in minerals like magnesium and calcium) than water in other countries, so for the best-tasting dashi, use a soft bottled water such as Volvic.

VEGETARIAN *DASHI*

MAKES SCANT 1.5 QUARTS (1.5 L)

Rinse the dried *shiitake* mushrooms once in water to help to remove the musty odor that arises from the drying process. You can also make a lighter *dashi* without shiitake mushrooms, using only *kombu* kelp. To do so, start from step 2 in the recipe.

INGREDIENTS

6 large dried shiitake mushrooms

2 cups (480 ml) water

1 to 2 pieces dried kombu kelp, each about 4 in. (10 cm) square

1 qt. (1 L) water

1   Briefly rinse the dried shiitake mushrooms in running cold water. Rehydrate in 1 cup water (see below). When the mushrooms are rehydrated, remove them. Pour the soaking water carefully through a strainer and reserve, leaving behind any broken bits and sand.

2   Combine the kombu and water in a pot over medium-low heat. The water should be approaching a boil after about 20 minutes (adjust the heat if the water looks like it's coming to a boil too soon or too slowly). Once the water comes to a boil, immediately turn off the heat. Remove the kombu.

3   Combine the shiitake mushroom stock with the kombu stock.

■ There are three ways to rehydrate dried mushrooms:
   Soak in 1 cup (240 ml) water in the refrigerator for 24 hours.
   Soak in 1 cup (240 ml) water at room temperature for 3 to 5 hours.
   Soak in 1 cup (240 ml) warm water for about 1 hour.

CHICKEN AND DRIED TOMATO BROTH

MAKES ABOUT 1.8 QUARTS (1.8 L)

Sprinkling the chicken with salt and letting it sit for one hour will triple or quadruple its flavorful amino acid content. Like dried shiitake mushrooms, dried tomatoes should be washed briefly in water to remove some of the off flavors that they acquire during the drying process.

INGREDIENTS

1 oz. (30 g) dried tomatoes

1 cup (240 ml) water

1 lb. (450 g) chicken breast, skinless

2 tsp salt

2 qts. (2 L) water

1   Briefly rinse the dried tomatoes in cold running water. Rehydrate in 1 cup water for 4 hours. Strain, reserving the soaking water.

2   Cut the chicken breast into thin slices and place in a bowl. Sprinkle with the salt, mix, and leave for 1 hour in refrigerator. The chicken will release its juices and then reabsorb them, becoming soft and a bit slippery.

3   Combine the water and chicken breast in a pot and bring to a simmer. Lower the heat, and maintain a bare simmer, with only one or two bubbles rising from the bottom of the pan, for 6 to 8 minutes. Skim the broth from time to time. Strain through a sieve.

4   Combine the dried tomato stock and the chicken breast stock.

Sauces

Here are recipes for some optional sauces: the tempura dipping sauce used on pages 32 and 34, *wasabi*-mayo sauce used on page 35, and soy-sesame sauce used on page 36. You don't need these sauces to make any of the recipes in this book; they're just for variation.

TEMPURA DIPPING SAUCE

MAKES ABOUT 1 CUP (240 ML)

The grated *daikon* radish and ginger cut through the oiliness of tempura and aid in digestion.

INGREDIENTS

2 Tbsp chicken broth

½ cup (120 ml) water

2 Tbsp soy sauce

1 Tbsp sugar

1 Tbsp grated daikon radish per serving

1 tsp grated ginger per serving

Combine all dipping sauce ingredients, except the daikon and ginger, in a small saucepan. Bring to a simmer, wait for 30 seconds, and remove from heat. Cool to room temperature. Pour into small individual serving bowls, place a mound of grated daikon radish in the sauce, and top with a little grated ginger. Just before eating, mix the grated daikon radish and ginger into the sauce.

WASABI-MAYO SAUCE

MAKES ABOUT ⅔ CUP (160 ML)

If this sauce has too much of a kick for you, reduce the *wasabi* to half the amount or less.

INGREDIENTS

¼ cup (60 ml) soy sauce

¼ cup plus 2 Tbsp (90 ml) mayonnaise

2 Tbsp wasabi paste

2 Tbsp sugar

Mix all ingredients together in a bowl.

SOY-SESAME SAUCE

MAKES ABOUT 1 CUP (240 ML)

Do not let the sauce come to a rolling boil at any point, or the cornstarch will break up and the sauce will not thicken.

INGREDIENTS

1 Tbsp sesame paste

3 Tbsp chicken broth

⅔ cup (160 ml) water

1 Tbsp soy sauce

⅓ cup (80 ml) Worcestershire sauce

1 ½ Tbsp cornstarch

Combine all ingredients in a small saucepan and bring to a simmer, stirring constantly. Continue to simmer gently until the sauce thickens. If you scoop some of the sauce up with a spoon, and it drops off the spoon like pea soup, then it's the right consistency.

abura-age deep-fried tofu Firm tofu cut into thin sheets and deep-fried.

Anaheim pepper An American variety of mild chili pepper. In Japan, *manganji* or *fushimi* peppers are used. Any mild variety can be substituted, or use ordinary bell peppers.

bonito flakes Dried flakes of *katsuo* (bonito or skipjack tuna) made by steaming, smoke-drying, and aging fillets of the fish until they are wood-hard, and then shredding them into flakes.

daikon radish A long white radish with a mild refreshing taste, good both raw (usually finely grated) and cooked.

dashi Japanese stock or broth used as a base for soups and sauces and to infuse umami into foods, usually made from dried kombu kelp and bonito flakes. There are other varieties of dashi made from dried small sardines, mackerel, and shiitake mushrooms. In fact, dashi can be made from any dried, umami-rich food: ham, dried mushrooms, dried tomatoes, and so on.

enoki mushrooms A long, white, noodle-shaped mushroom with a mild flavor.

escabeche Fish and vegetables that have been deep-fried and marinated in vinegar, called *nambanzuke* in Japanese. Like tempura, escabeche came to Japan with the first Portuguese and Spanish explorers hundreds of years ago.

ikura salmon roe Cleaned and salted salmon roe. "Ikura" is originally a Russian word meaning fish roe.

kabocha squash A Japanese variety of winter squash, like a pumpkin but firmer and less watery. Kabocha has bright yellow-orange flesh and a hard, but thin and edible, dark green rind. The rind is often partially peeled to show off the contrast between the green skin and orange flesh.

kamaboko A kind of fish sausage or fish cake made by grinding the meat of several varieties of fish and mixing it with seasonings, curing it, and steaming it into different shapes and textures.

kanikama Imitation crab legs made from kamaboko. Some kanikama products have real crab meat blended in with the kamaboko.

kimpira Shredded vegetables sautéed and seasoned with soy sauce, sugar (or *mirin*), chili peppers and sesame seeds. Burdock root and carrot is a common combination, but there are many variations.

konnyaku A very stiff, nearly flavorless white jelly made by grinding the root of the konnyaku (konjac) plant and coagulating it with calcium hydroxide. Another type, grayish brown in color, contains *hijiki* seaweed. Rich in fiber with almost no calories, konnyaku is sold in slabs or shaped into noodles called *shirataki*.

kombu kelp A variety of giant kelp that is dried and used for dashi. Most Japanese kombu is grown off the coast of Hokkaido, the country's northernmost main island.

miso An intensely flavorful paste made from soybeans and rice or other grains, steamed and fermented with salt. Full of umami, miso comes in hundreds of local varieties.

panko bread crumbs Coarse white bread crumbs used for deep-frying in Japanese food. Panko is lighter than other commercial bread crumbs because it is made from bread without crusts.

rice vinegar Vinegar made by fermenting steamed rice with acetic acid bacteria. Slow-brewed rice vinegar is not merely sour, but has umami and other complex flavors and aromas. Essential for making sushi.

sake An alcoholic beverage made by double-fermenting cooked rice; first to turn the starches into sugars, and then to turn the sugars into alcohol.

shichimi spice powder   A Japanese spice mix often made by combining chili pepper flakes, sesame seeds, poppy seeds, *sansho* pepper, *nori* (seaweed), dried orange peel and other spices. There are many variations.

shiitake mushrooms   A mushroom native to China with a meaty, earthy flavor. Fresh shiitake are grilled, deep-fried, sautéed or stewed. Dried shiitake are used to make dashi.

shirataki   See **konnyaku**.

shiso leaves   A Japanese herb related to mint and basil, with an aroma like basil, but fresher and grassier. There is also a purple variety with a slightly different aroma that is used to color and flavor pickled vegetables.

soba buckwheat noodles   Noodles made from buckwheat flour. Different grades of soba are available, containing varying proportions of buckwheat and wheat flour.

soy sauce   A liquid condiment made by fermenting steamed soybeans with roasted wheat and salt. Like other Japanese essential seasonings such as rice vinegar and sake, good, slow-brewed soy sauce is mild but profound, full of umami and other flavors and aromas.

tempura   Seasonal vegetables and seafood battered with flour, egg, and water and deep-fried in hot oil, eaten with sea salt or with a dipping sauce based on soy sauce and dashi. Brought to Japan by the Portuguese almost five hundred years ago.

teriyaki   A grilling technique in which fish or meat is basted and glazed with a mixture of sugar, soy sauce and sake while grilling or sautéing to add flavor and create a glossy shine.

tofu   Soy milk that has been coagulated into a dense, protein-rich solid. Good-quality tofu is tender and milky, not watery or rubbery, so look around a little for the best tofu you can find.

umami   A fifth taste, scientifically discovered in Japan but really known everywhere, sometimes called "savoriness." Umami receptors are located in the back of the tongue and are stimulated by free amino acids found in meats, seaweed, and certain vegetables like tomatoes and mushrooms. Curing or drying foods enhances their natural umami.

wasabi   The root of a plant that grows near pure mountain streams, ground into a paste and eaten as a condiment on many foods, most notably sushi and sashimi. The paste has a hot, refreshing pungency, like strong mustard or horseradish. Wasabi sold in paste or powder form is usually mixed with horseradish, but is an acceptable substitute.

yaki-tofu   Tofu pressed with a very hot grill to create a firmer texture and blackened grill lines, used for sautéing and in hot pots.

INDEX

Bold type indicates an item that is defined in the glossary (pp. 106–107).

CONVERSIONS

LENGTH

Imperial	Metric
⅛ in.	3 mm
¼ in.	6 mm
½ in.	1 cm
1 in.	2.5 cm
1 ½ in.	4 cm
2 in.	5 cm
2 ½ in.	6 cm
3 in.	7.5 cm
4 in.	10 cm
5 in.	13 cm
6 in.	15 cm
8 in.	20 cm

TEMPERATURE

Fahrenheit (ºF)	Celsius (ºC)
250	120
275	130
300	150
325	160
340	170
350	180
375	190
390	200
400	210
425	220
450	230
475	245

VOLUME

U.S.	Metric
⅛ tsp	0.5 ml
¼ tsp	1 ml
½ tsp	2.5 ml
¾ tsp	4 ml
1 tsp	5 ml
1 Tbsp (3 tsp)	15 ml
¼ cup (4 Tbsp)	60 ml
⅓ cup	80 ml
½ cup	120 ml
⅔ cup	160 ml
¾ cup	180 ml
1 cup	240 ml
1 ¼ cups	300 ml
1 ½ cups	360 ml
2 cups	480 ml
2 ½ cups	600 ml
3 cups	720 ml
4 cups (1 qt.)	1,000 ml (1 L)
1 gallon (4 qts.)	4 L

WEIGHT

Ounces	Grams
¼ oz.	7 g
½ oz.	15 g
⅔ oz.	20 g
1 oz.	30 g
2 oz.	60 g
3 oz.	85 g
4 oz.	120 g
5 oz.	140 g
6 oz.	170 g
7 oz.	200 g
8 oz.	230 g
9 oz.	255 g
10 oz.	280 g
11 oz.	310 g
12 oz.	340 g
14 oz.	400 g
16 oz. (1 lb.)	450 g
2 lbs.	900 g
2 ¼ lbs.	1,000 g (1 kg)

The author and publisher would like to thank Chisako Hori
and Masahito Tsuji of Kikunoi for their gracious cooperation.

Contributing Editor: Noriko Yokota
Translations: Derek Wilcox
Copyediting: Katherine Heins and Matthew Cotterill

（英文版）楽しく簡単 和のおかず
Japanese Home Cooking with Master Chef Murata

2010年6月25日　第1刷発行

著　者　村田吉弘
撮　影　齋藤 明
発行者　廣田浩二
発行所　講談社インターナショナル株式会社
　　　　〒112-8652 東京都文京区音羽1-17-14
　　　　電話　03-3944-6493（編集部）
　　　　　　　03-3944-6492（マーケティング部・業務部）
　　　　ホームページ　www.kodansha-intl.com
印刷・製本所　大日本印刷株式会社